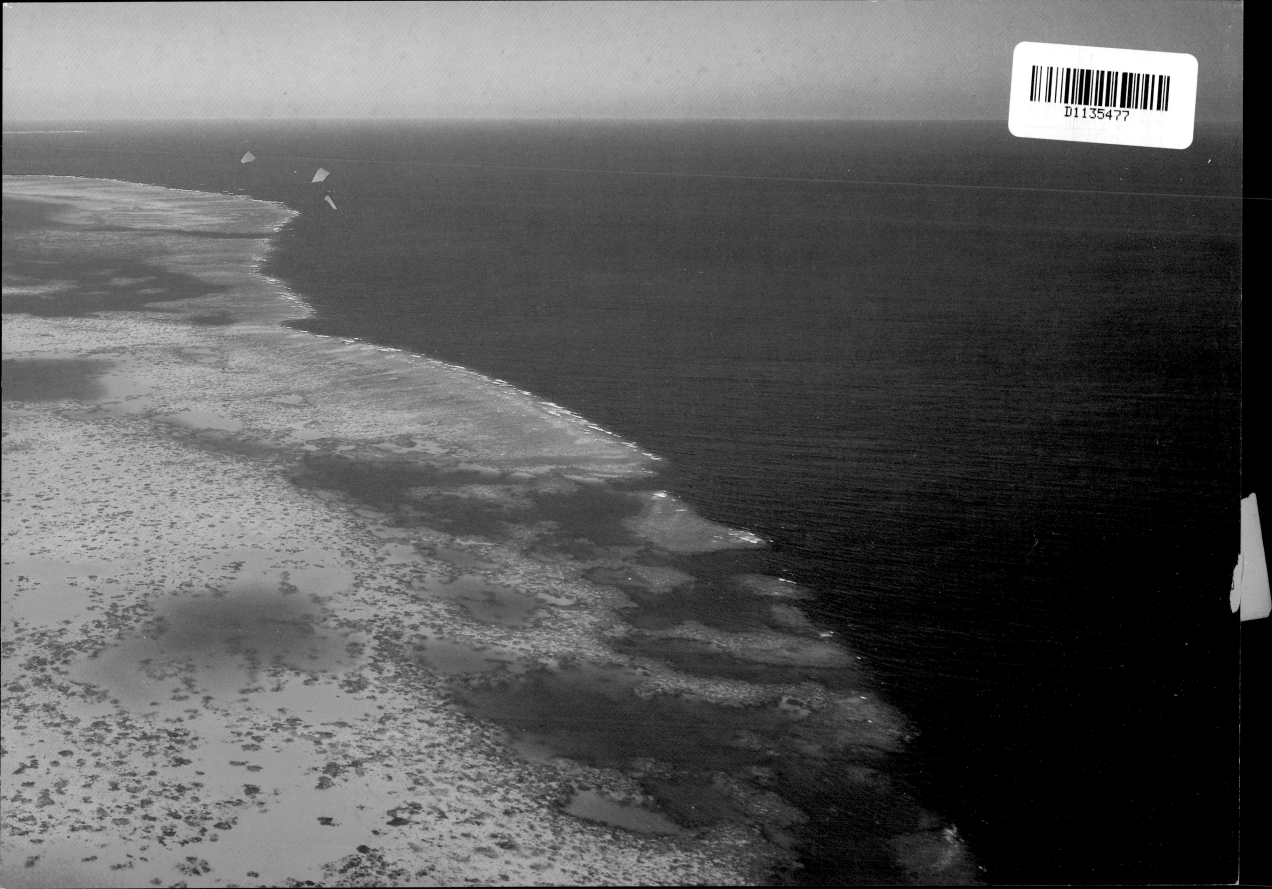

The Great South Land

Tierra Austrialia Del Espiritu Santo - The Great South Land of the Holy Spirit

PANOGRAPHS® BY KEN DUNCAN

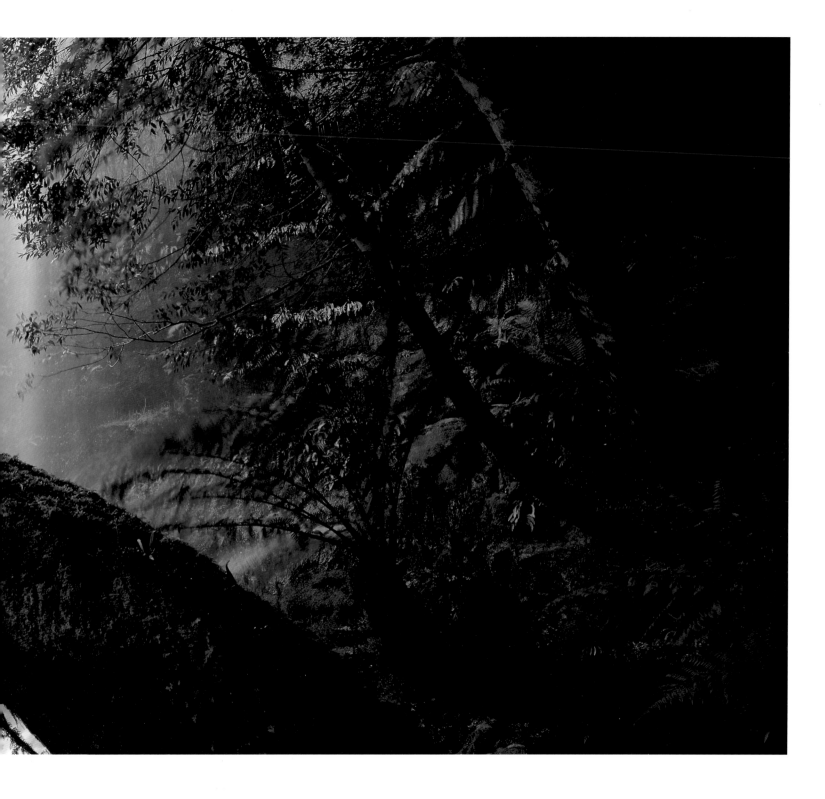

The Great South Land

THE GREAT SOUTH LAND

FIRST PUBLISHED IN 1997

BY KEN DUNCAN PANOGRAPHS® PTY LIMITED

ACN 050 235 606

PO BOX 15, WAMBERAL NSW 2260, AUSTRALIA.

TELEPHONE: (02) 4367 6777.

COPYRIGHT PHOTOGRAPHY AND TEXT:

© KEN DUNCAN 1997

DESIGNED BY GOOD CATCH DESIGN.

TEXT BY KEN DUNCAN

EDITED BY OWEN SALTER.

COLOUR SEPARATIONS BY PURESCRIPT.

PRINTED BY EVERBEST PRINTING CO.,LTD.,

REPRINTED 1998, 1999

THE NATIONAL LIBRARY OF AUSTRALIA

CATALOGUING-IN-PUBLICATION ENTRY:

DUNCAN, KEN

AUSTRALIA WIDE: THE GREAT SOUTH LAND

INCLUDES INDEX

ISBN 0 9586681 3 2

1. AUSTRALIA - PICTORIAL WORKS. I TITLE

994.0650222

THE KEN DUNCAN GALLERIES:

73 GEORGE STREET, THE ROCKS, SYDNEY, NSW.

TELEPHONE (02) 9241 3460.

5740 OAK ROAD, MATCHAM, NSW.

TELEPHONE (02) 4367 6777.

SHOP U6 SOUTHGATE, MELBOURNE, VICTORIA.

TELEPHONE (03) 9686 8022.

OR VISIT THE KEN DUNCAN GALLERY ON-LINE

http://www.kenduncan.com

Acknowledgements

Above

Wallace Hut, Falls Creek, Victoria

would like to offer my sincere thanks to the companies who have supported me in the production of this book. I have worked with these companies over many years, and know they are strongly committed to this Great South Land.

May they all reap abundantly as they have sown.

Special thanks to my wife Pamela, my daughter Jessica, all my fantastic staff, Barry and Lyn Follett, Jim and Neta Duncan, Jean McKimmin, Victoria Jefferys, Peter Morley, Paul Thomas, Dennis Harding, Alan Grosse, and many others who have helped along the way.

God bless you all.

Contents

8
Western Australia
The Golden State

34
Queensland
The Sunshine State

58
South Australia
The Festival State

78
New South Wales
The First State

106
Victoria
The Garden State

136
Northern Territory
The Outback

162
Tasmania
The Holiday Isle

AUSTRALIA WIDE

Foreword

Above
Pine Valley, Cradle Mountain-Lake St Clair National Park, Tasmania

Australia is a place of immense beauty with a striking diversity of landscapes. Whether it is the extraordinary harsh expanse of the remote Kimberley region or the verdant green of Tasmania's rainforests, this country contains a phenomenal range of unique natural environment. Australia has always been a settled continent and we are indebted to the Aboriginal people, whose connection with the land was of critical importance to their beliefs and social customs, and, as well, to succeeding generations of conservation minded Australians, who have seen this natural heritage as worth preserving. Our country is remarkable for having a high proportion of internationally recognised regions of natural and cultural significance, like Uluru and The Great Barrier Reef, and fortunate to have a photographer of the skill of Ken Duncan to record these treasures.

As the century draws to a close many people have come to believe, rightly I think, that there is an urgent need to reverse our priorities to ensure that there is a sufficiently healthy ecosystem for human communities to inhabit, not only because nature nourishes our bodies but also because it is a balm for our souls. Yet tragically, many of the locations that Ken has recorded with his customary keen eye and acute sense of the elements of a good photo, are under direct threat from the never ending drive to take profit from the land without regard for the consequences. This is a challenge we all face and so my hope is that the character and the essence of the sites and scenes captured in *"The Great South Land"* inspire us and remain with us always.

PETER GARRETT, MIDNIGHT OIL

Introduction

Above
St Luke's, Mullengandra, New South Wales

Overleaf
"Let There Be Light", Avoca, New South Wales

This is a book for the heart, not the head. In our special country of Australia there is a presence that can only be experienced in the spirit. A small rural church nestling among wildflowers is symbolic of the fountain of spiritual strength that I believe lies in the very fabric of this land. Ever since Europeans first set foot in Australia, they have been fascinated, baffled and over-awed by its wild beauty. Aboriginal people before them knew how to be nurtured by the land and how to nurture it in return. There is Life in the land—the Creator of the universe is here.

Out in the wilderness, in the forest or desert, there is a wonderful order and peace that recharges the human soul. That tranquillity blows like a fresh breeze through this nation. It is the breeze of the Spirit. You can't own it. But if you humble yourself and trim your sails, it will take you on a great adventure. I hope you feel the ruffle of that breeze in these photographs of our Great South Land.

This book is dedicated to the Holy Spirit. May Your soothing oil anoint this land, that unity may reign.

Ken Duncan.

The Golden State

WESTERN AUSTRALIA

There's a lot of adventure to be had in Western Australia. Some of the state's most spectacular locations are so far off the beaten track that it takes days to walk in to them. Some you can only get to by air or boat. Some haven't even been discovered yet.

Much of Western Australia is harsh and barren land. Three of Australia's major deserts, as well as the pancake-flat Nullarbor Plain, spread out for hundreds of thousands of kilometres. In the far north lies the Kimberley, larger than many small countries, an area of geological wonders, massive cattle stations and climatic extremes. It still hides remote places where you can walk and know that very few white people, if any, have ever been there.

This outback country produces a breed of men and women who are resilient in the extreme: self-reliant, resourceful and tough. Straight-forward, too—you don't hear many words from them, but their rugged lives speak volumes. Some of the folk I most respect make their homes in the wilderness of Western Australia.

To the south and south-west, marvellous beaches and majestic karri forests spread out along the coasts. With their temperate climate and surf-loving crowds they are a world away from life up north, but the people have an air of optimism and durability not unlike their outback cousins.

I have a personal link with Western Australia that makes it special to me. My parents lived and worked with Aboriginal people in the Kimberley before I was born. Whenever I return to its splendid isolation, I find myself deeply humbled. The awesome landscape makes me realise I'm not in control. All I can do is let it wash over me.

Whenever we have the courage to encounter the natural world as it is, not manipulate it to be what we want it to be, it will inevitably nourish our soul.

Previous Page
Piccaninny Creek, Purnululu National Park

As the sun rises, the awe-inspiring domes of the Bungle Bungle massif are reflected with unwavering precision in the waters of a pool at the end of Piccaninny Gorge. Weathered over millennia into amazing formations of banded stone, the domes rise like a stupendous city in the remote north-east of the state. This pool, photographed at the end of the wet season, is likely to last only a month or so before the arid heat dries it to bare rock. But in the meantime it awaits the dawning of a new day, adding tranquillity to the harsh world it so delicately mirrors.

Bell Creek Falls, the Kimberley

Silky water flowing over Bell Creek Falls presents a sharp contrast to the armour-plate roughness of Kimberley rock. The spring-fed Isdell River—like most water in the Kimberley—is crystal clear, and swimming holes above and below these falls give welcome relief to visitors. When bathed in explosive noon sunlight, scenes like this seduce photographers with their beauty; but here the afterglow of sunset captures a subtler, wilder mood.

Overleaf
The evocative lines of sand dunes near Eucla follow an ancient geometry.

Above
The Arch, Purnululu National Park

Rising from the scrubby desert plain, a natural arch large enough to drive a truck through displays a stately and powerful grandeur. Standing over fifteen metres (50 feet) high and splashed with rich earth colours like some gigantic rock painting, it is just one of the countless hidden treasures of Purnululu—a priceless art gallery set up by the Creator to display some of his most breathtaking works.

Right
"Dawn of Creation", Mitchell Falls

All night while camping here at Mitchell Falls in the western Kimberley we were surrounded by fires lit by National Parks authorities to aid the germination of bush seeds—a form of environmental care practised by Aborigines for millennia. As the smoke filtered the early morning light with lovely evenness, the colours of rock and water began to glow. Now, as I recall this unrepeatable moment, I think of a line from an old Eagles' song—"Call some place Paradise and kiss it goodbye"—and I say a prayer for the preservation of such unique wilderness.

A fabulous gallery of roses adorns the front garden of Sarah Levy's small cottage in Boyanup, south of Perth. Sarah and her husband called it "our little Eden"—a joy-filled sanctuary created through many years of love and attention.

Behind the middle drop of Mitchell Falls is a cavern, where the noise of falling water is deafening but the view is magical. I call this shot "Beyond the Veil" because it reminds me that sometimes we've got to push aside the curtains that blinker our sight to get a clearer vision of what's really there.

Like an army of terra cotta figures, the limestone pillars of the Pinnacles, 245 km (152 miles) north of Perth, tell a silent tale of aeons of geological weathering. Standing to attention in a rippling sea of sand, they look like the long-dead inhabitants of a barren moonscape— except for the tiny bushes clinging cheekily to existence at their feet, speaking simultaneously of the fragility and tenacity of life.

Seldom have I felt like renaming a place more than this idyllic sheltered cove on Western Australia's south coast, east of Esperance. With water so clear and sand so white, it would be hard to imagine anything less hell-like.

Above
Echidna Chasm, Purnululu National Park

The trunks of Livistona palms in narrow Echidna Chasm stretch eagerly towards a typically azure Australian sky. Such trees huddle together oasis-like in a number of chasms of the Bungle Bungle Ranges, their rich green foliage a striking contrast to the arid surroundings.

The water at the top of these falls in the remote north Kimberley is pure and wonderful to drink; the water at the bottom is brackish and home to some very serious crocodiles. Just 12 km (7.5 miles) from the Timor Sea, the falls are one of the most untouched places in Australia. Free from the distractions of humanity, the sense of God's presence here for me is simply overwhelming.

LAND

The colours and textures of a simple working building suddenly come alive as sunlight filters through an old shearing shed at Kookynie, 200 km (125 miles) north of Kalgoorlie. Soon the walls will echo again with the sounds of another shearing season—the frightened bleating of animals and the voices of men who thrive in a world of hard work, tall tales and steady mateship.

The Fitzroy River, meandering with dry season docility, rises in the wet season to flood the surrounding grey sand banks and reach 10 metres (32 feet) and more up the cliffs of Geikie Gorge. Abounding in caves and lovely natural limestone sculptures, this area looks particularly spectacular, as here, at sunrise.

The Sunshine State

Queensland is a land of fantasy. Whether it be lounging on a sun-drenched sand cay surrounded by turquoise water, fishing for black marlin in the Coral Sea or snorkelling on the incomparable Great Barrier Reef, thousands look to Queensland to fulfil their dreams—even if only for a holiday fortnight.

Even locals, who are a little less starry-eyed, revel in a carefree lifestyle of barbeque, beach and bare feet, a combination that makes their state outstandingly sociable and hospitable. Sunshine, of course, is Queensland's secret. There are beaches in Queensland where the sand is so white and reflective that your skin burns from above and below!

But Queensland isn't all tropical paradise. Over the Great Dividing Range, the vast and barren outback stretches to the Northern Territory border. Up north on the Cape York Peninsula, where the roads are all four-wheel drive tracks and rain-swollen rivers can wash your vehicle away, the tropical paradise becomes a gut-wrenching tropical adventure.

I have very fond memories of people in Queensland. On one journey, sick and lost, our party limped into the outback town of Burketown, with one vehicle under tow and the motor of the other roped in because the engine mounts had snapped. Although we were total strangers, the local publicans, Tex and Lorraine, cared for us like family. That's something you often find in the bush. Away from the suspicion-inducing pressures of city life, people are free to give of themselves with fewer reservations.

In fact, being out in the wilderness has a way of measuring us for what we really are. The bush is the great equaliser; it doesn't differentiate between a prince and a pauper. You can take with you as many props of "civilisation" as you want, but out in the unknown you'll never have enough to deal with every situation. That's where the depth of a person is revealed.

Right
Pandanus Palms, Mapoon

In a dance as elegant as any ballet, palm fronds sway in the gentle ocean breeze to farewell the passing day. Here, on the secluded shores of the Gulf of Carpentaria, evening arrives with a magnificent display of pastel light.

Previous Page
"Majestic Beauty", Millaa Millaa Falls

With their roots deep in rich volcanic soil, the tree ferns of the Atherton Tablelands thrive on the kind of tropical rainfall that keeps innumerable waterfalls flowing all year. I just love water—the greenery it brings, the wondrous life. To me it's like God's love pouring down.

Left
Mail plane, Musgrave Station

Cape York Peninsula is one of the few places in the world where you can stop at a petrol bowser and have a plane pull in behind you. With mail bags peering out the rear window, this aircraft demonstrates a common form of transport in an area with very few roads.

Overleaf
"Crystal Clear Waters", Whitehaven Beach

More than 70 islands crowd into the Whitsunday Passage between the Queensland coast and the Great Barrier Reef, and none has a beach more exquisite than this. Pure silicon sand, pellucid waters and gentle lapping waves draw visitors by the thousand to a spot that almost defines the word "idyllic".

Many people dream of sailing away. Here, inside the Great Barrier Reef, protected from the swells of the southern Pacific Ocean by a 2300 km (1430 miles) long coral bastion, a white boat with sails furled sits at anchor. Lying here with the whole world before it, it seems to bob in a sea of serenity; but to reach its place of rest this craft has had to negotiate treacherous reef waters and weather many storms. Realising our dream to sail away is often harder than we think—but what an adventure!

Like slaves waving palm branches to cool oriental kings, the fan palms of Cape Tribulation hold their wheel-like foliage aloft to give shade from the draining tropical heat. Named in 1770 by a somewhat despondent Captain Cook after he ran aground on nearby Endeavour Reef, this area is one of Australia's richest rainforest habitats. How regal one feels walking beneath such a verdant canopy, bathed in the softness of the light as it plays in the early morning mist.

Hinchinbrook Island is a spectacular wilderness of granite mountains, impenetrable jungle and thick mangrove swamps like those lining the shores of North Zoe Creek. The Janzsia, a classic white trimaran, has moored here overnight, and now at first light it is rewarded with a vista of alluring and softly brooding beauty. Although its National Park status should ensure its sanctity, Hinchinbrook continues to be the focus of developers' dreams. I just hope they don't ruin the character of this marvellously wild place.

Faint traces of human presence cross the sand as Noah Beach greets a new morning. On this beach, two of the least spoiled wildernesses left on planet Earth meet—the ocean, with its untameable power and vast mystery, and the rainforest, so brimming with life that new plant and animal species continue to be discovered there. Part of the Wet Tropics World Heritage Area, the region has been mercifully saved from commercial logging. But now it faces another challenge: how to cope with the impact of thousands of visitors coming to see this phenomenally special world.

Right
"Paradise", Fantome Island

With Palm Island in the background crowned by clouds, and a pristine beach washed by cool aqua water, this scene seemed so impossibly lovely I couldn't resist calling it "Paradise". To me it epitomises what Queensland is about. When I'm busy I often stop to look at this shot and imagine I'm there!

Previous Page
The Lions Den Hotel, Helenvale

Marks left by a long stream of patrons adorn the walls of one of Australia's memorable pubs, a watering hole on the road from Cooktown to Cape York. Travellers stop here to get information about 'the Track' as well as share a friendly beer. A typical bush collection of rocks, skulls and pickled snakes sits on the piano, while an ominous warning about "dunnys" (toilets) and a multitude of business cards help make this a jovial launching pad for the adventure to the continent's Top.

Left
Butcher's Creek, near Cloncurry

Situated in the state's west out towards Mount Isa, Cloncurry is the site of Australia's highest recorded temperature—55°C (131°F). This oven-like environment ensures that creek beds stay waterless for most of the year. Then, after months of dust and dryness and shimmering haze, the spring rains come, and thirsty dirt bowls become streams of refreshment. Meanwhile, the river gums cling on through all seasons, dependent not on the vagaries of casual showers but on the steady supply of hidden water underground.

Above
Fern fronds as delicate as lace decorate Nandroya Falls, Palmerston National Park.

Overleaf
Fruit Bat Falls, Heathland Reserve, Cape York Peninsula

Right
Bushfires near Weipa

I wanted to capture the wonderful crispness of Eliot Creek rolling over Fruit Bat Falls, but after hours of shooting I still felt dissatisfied. Suddenly it occurred to me I needed to see the scene in a fresh way. Up to my neck in the fresh, translucent water I finally managed to catch what I was after—with my last shot. How often we miss the very thing we're looking for because we're not prepared to look at things from a different perspective!

With a furnace glow, a small scrub fire burns outwards in a circle of death and life. Death comes to the old undergrowth, but in its place new shoots break through. In a hard land where fire is part of the natural cycle, life must be resilient—like the small palm tree standing here miraculously unscathed.

SOUTH AUSTRALIA

The Festival State

The subtle beauty of South Australia is not always easy to find. Geographically the state is mostly desert or semi-desert, and it's hard to reach many of the loveliest places. Aesthetically, too, the beauty can be elusive, unwilling to surrender its delights to casual acquaintances. To appreciate South Australia's landscapes you must take time to build a relationship with them.

Situated between the populous eastern states and the go-it-alone West, South Australia has often been treated as little more than a road and rail junction to elsewhere. The reason for this neglect is obvious: four-fifths of the state is arid and very unwelcoming. But the south, with

the green slopes and valleys of the Adelaide Hills, the rugged coastlines of the Yorke Peninsula and the unspoilt isolation of Kangaroo Island, has great charms.

The Flinders Ranges, too, contain some of the great scorched landscapes of Australia. There you feel the deep resilience of life in a place where the sun is an unremitting dictator.

As if to counter the harshness of the land, South Australians have developed a leisurely approach to life that is proud of what it has achieved but not overblown with pretension. Every two years, they let their hair down for the world-renowned Adelaide Arts Festival that

gives the state its "Festival" slogan.

Deep down, though, I think South Australia is a battler's state. Perhaps more people have gone under trying to scratch a living from the barren soil here than anywhere else in Australia. The abandoned cottages that dot the countryside speak of the hope and heartbreak of men and women who have poured their lives into their dreams, only to see them blow away with the dust.

They are a stark reminder that real wealth is more than temporal, earthly gain. Only heavenly treasures last, and these come from living for something greater than just our own desires.

A perfect wave is caught for an instant as it nears the end of its journey from the Southern Ocean, preparing to cast itself at the feet of the dark, cragged cliffs of Yorke Peninsula. In a way this photograph came by accident. My normal camera broke down and I had to use a more cumbersome one. But the second camera had one advantage: it was much better at freezing action. This experience taught me that sometimes when things go wrong, it can jolt you out of your comfort zone and force you to stretch yourself, with great rewards.

Above
Dunes at Gunyah Beach, Coffin Bay National Park, rippling like a windblown sea.

Overleaf
Flinders Ranges

Like a Hans Heysen painting come alive, an old shed stands beneath the rocky heights of some of Australia's most awesomely rugged scenery. Alive with the pioneer spirit of the men and women who tried to tame this fierce terrain, this scene also captures the intricate blending of range and landscape that creates the intimate and subtle moods of the Flinders Ranges.

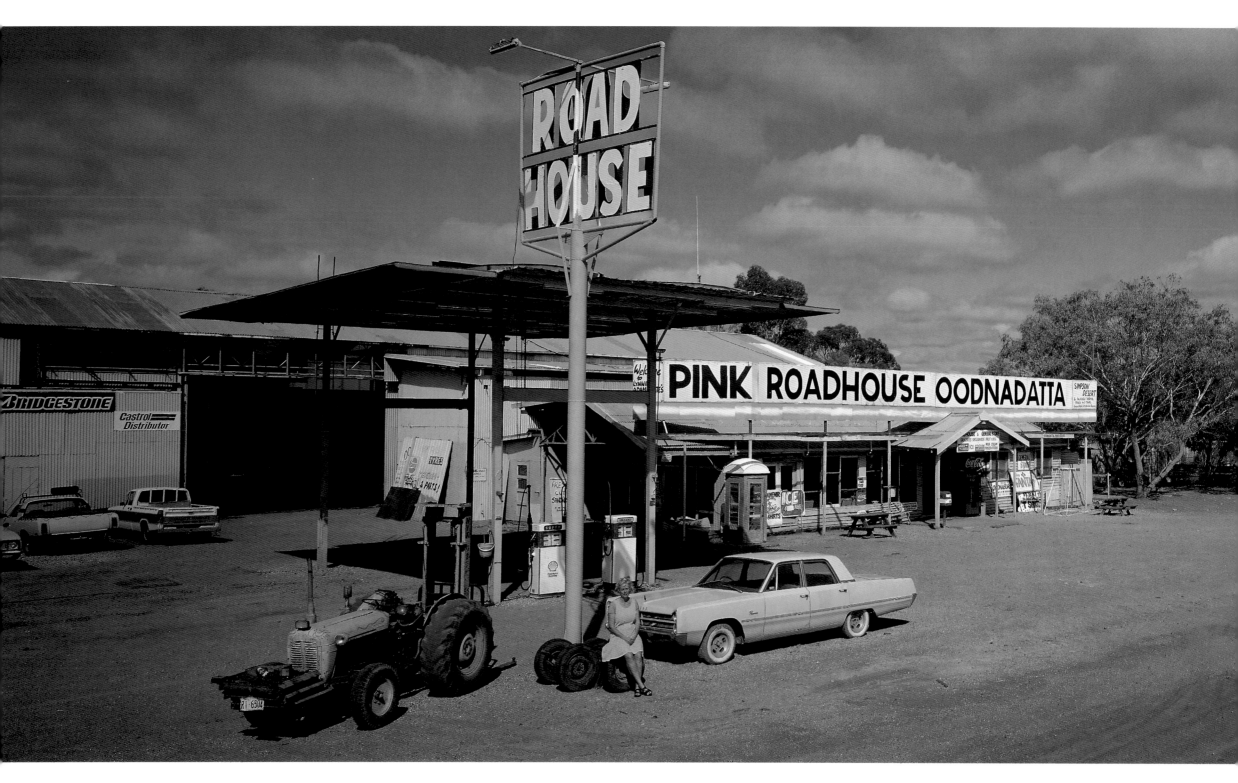

Pink-toned Lynnie Plate, co-owner with husband Adam of the Pink Roadhouse, welcomes travellers on the famous Oodnadatta Track, a 620 km (385 miles) dirt road across some of the state's most drab and arid territory. Formerly an important stop on the Ghan railway line between Adelaide and Alice Springs, Oodnadatta is now 400 metres (1300 feet) of endearing oddness centred on this marvellous establishment. Rising from the ground like some surreal dream, it is a tribute to one of the most essential qualities for survival in the bush—a sense of humour.

Right
Steam Engine Roundhouse, Peterborough

Years of neglect may have leeched the glory from this old engine, but its character is still intact, waiting under layers of rust and dirt to be resurrected. The remnant of a once proud fleet, it is now the object of restoration efforts. It is vital to preserve memories of our past to provide foundations for our future.

Overleaf
"Daybreak Sentinel", Flinders Ranges

Like the seven-branched lampstand that lit the ancient Jewish temple, a grass tree, venerable with age and solitude, stands silhouetted against the beautiful morning glow of God's light. In the background, the walls of Wilpena Pound stand as a crown testifying to the majesty of a new day.

Left
Kangaroo Beach, Kangaroo Island

Sometimes in life you can aim for one thing only to be unexpectedly presented with something far better. When I asked a local farmer to direct me to Snug Cove on the north coast of Kangaroo Island, he offered instead to show me his own property—and led me to this breathtaking little bay. Surrounded by straw-coloured hills that autumn rains will soon turn to green, this scene made Snug Cove, when I finally saw it, seem nothing by comparison.

Above
Dolphin Bay, Innes National Park

Rocks stained red by algae crowd the shores of blue-watered Dolphin Bay. Situated at the south-western tip of Yorke Peninsula, the area was made a National Park in 1965 and abounds in bird life. With excellent swimming, fishing, diving and surfing, it is a popular holiday destination for city-weary folk from Adelaide and dust-weary folk from the outback.

Right
Bunyeroo Valley, Flinders Ranges National Park

Dorothy McKellar's famous poem about Australia begins with the words "I love a sunburnt country", and you couldn't get much more sunburnt than this. The land seems to smoulder as the rising sun starts to gather heat, creating an illusion of barrenness. In reality the hills and bluffs are liberally sprinkled with a thriving diversity of vegetation.

Overleaf
The Remarkables, Flinders Chase National Park, Kangaroo Island

Against a flower pink sky, the scooped indentations and sandpaper texture of the Remarkable rock carvings stand out as the masterpieces they truly are. Many sculptors would give almost anything to be able to create such works of art, and here they are, just lying around for anyone to view—for free.

NEW SOUTH WALES

The First State

The "splendour of creation" is certainly on display in New South Wales. As I waited one morning for sunrise on a north Sydney beach, I had no idea that one of my photographs would reveal the shape of a huge angel in a wave, its wings spread wide. It was just one of the many surprises that lie hidden in this great part of Australia.

New South Wales is certainly the state with the beach frontage—1600 kilometres (995 miles) of Pacific shoreline that ensure the New South Wales lifestyle largely revolves around the water. Most of the population live along the coast, centred in Sydney, the oldest, largest and most sophisticated city in Australia. But New South Wales has natural wonders that rival the famed icons of the Opera House and the Harbour Bridge. Even the arid western plains, where only a handful of people keep the kangaroos and emus company, have their own simmering attractiveness.

Many people don't realise the diversity of landscape in New South Wales, from northern rainforest through river country to the southern snow fields and the desolate outback in the west. Experiencing these remote areas brings an important balance to the full-on life of the coastal sprawl. Speed doesn't necessarily equal quality of life.

Nor does material prosperity gained at the expense of destroying our fragile world. In New South Wales, pristine old growth forests are being logged to satisfy the dictates of short-term gain. I believe we have already gone too far and cannot afford to lose even one more old growth tree.

We have been made the caretakers of this planet, but what kind of job are we doing? We need to look beyond what we can selfishly grab for today and focus on the future. The creation is standing up like that angelic wave and crying out, "Wake up! Wake up!" If we don't listen, we will pay a terrible price.

Previous Page
Sheather's Wharf, Koolewong

Above
The world holds its breath in the morning mist of Mangrove Mountain, north of Gosford.

The peaceful glow of twilight lingers on the clinker-built boats of Sheather's Wharf, giving their pencil-box colours an exotic feel against the wharf's business-like austerity. To catch this mood on film required a five minute exposure, and no sooner had I finished than a water skier shattered the stillness. Such perfect timing always makes me aware that I am being "helped" to capture the beauty of God's creation.

Above
As at the dawn of creation, life explodes in all directions in Dorrigo National Park.

Overleaf
Snowball Farm, on the road to Gundagai

In the frantic speed of the modern world, people often race past beautiful things and never notice them. Right beside the busy Hume Highway, this old timber farmhouse sits in a brilliant field of Paterson's Curse, probably Australia's most famous weed. To me it is symbolic of the transience of man's dreams—his grand ambitions overtaken by a field of flowers.

Left
Round up, Glenworth Valley

Fresh from a night free of the saddle, the horses of Glenworth Valley riding farm at Peats Ridge, Central Coast, bolt across a creek towards the main corral. From there they will spend the day carrying riders across one of the largest free range riding areas in the country—children and adults feeling a little of the country's history and dreaming of emulating the exploits of the most legendary rider of all, the Man from Snowy River.

Above
Macarthurs' Homestead, Belgenny Farm, Camden

In 1805 John Macarthur, an army officer and farming pioneer, established a sheep farm 50 km (30 miles) south-west of Sydney. Going on to produce wool that rivalled the best in the world, Macarthur is today acknowledged as the father of Australian agriculture. If you visit his property soon after sunrise, when the ghostly shapes of buildings have just emerged from the mist, it's hard not to feel you've woken up in another century.

Waiting for a breeze to set its cogs clanking, a windmill in western New South Wales is the only connection between thirsty crops and the plentiful artesian reservoirs that lie deep beneath the crusty ground. In terms of rainfall, Australia is virtually the driest continent on earth (second only to Antarctica), yet enormous tracts of the country are blessed with abundant underground water—even the Nullarbor Plain.

There's such a happiness in acres of brilliant sunflowers turned in unison to greet the dawn sun. For me, they teach a lesson in the importance of keeping focussed on the true source of light and not getting sidetracked by distractions. And of course, as they focus on the light, their own precious beauty is illuminated.

Left
"Golden Sands", Narrabeen Beach

Like gold dust sprinkled around, the gilded sands of Narrabeen Beach play host at daybreak to three fishermen and a million footprints. Immensely popular for swimming and surfing, Sydney's coast contains some of the most beautiful and extensive city beaches in the world. In fact, Australian beaches generally are among the best anywhere, with sands ranging from gold to brown, red, grey or white—even rainbow!

Overleaf
Geehi Hut, Murray River, Kosciuszko National Park

Sunlight sparkles on the headwaters of the Murray River, flowing down from the melting snows of Australia's highest peak, Mt Kosciuszko. Faced by extremes of weather and isolation, the pioneers who unlocked the Snowy Mountains grappled with daily hardships that we who live in the relative softness of the modern era can barely imagine. Staying in touch with what our forefathers went through helps us keep our own troubles in perspective.

Spread out like a fabled lost world, the crags and valleys of the Warrumbungles look like a hiding place for dinosaurs. The jagged spires and domes, formed from solidified lava that long ago exploded from the earth, brood over a world that still seems strangely prehistoric.

Previous Page
The Three Sisters, Katoomba, The Blue Mountains

One of New South Wales' leading icons, the Three Sisters rise against the deep blue distance of the Jamison Valley. The gnarled formations take their name from an Aboriginal story, which relates how a tribal leader turned his three daughters to stone during a battle to protect them from their enemies, only to be killed before he could return them to life.

Right
"Pastel Sunrise", Freshwater Beach

Morning explodes in a firework display of colour above one of Sydney's northern beaches. The surfer who has wandered into the photograph seems stunned into immobility, contemplating the prospect of riding the waves under a canopy of such grandeur. I hope he's also pondering the power of the One who so effortlessly tosses off this kind of stunning artwork every day.

Above
"The Power and the Glory", Avoca

There's nothing better than sitting in front of a wild ocean. As each wave hits it takes away some of the dross of our lives.

Overleaf
Sunrise over the Pacific

Black clouds above a boiling sea threaten rain, but against all expectation they emit instead cascades of light.

Right
Lower Ebor Falls, Dorrigo National Park

Australia is full of marvellous waterfalls, but one mistake that we photographers sometimes make is to focus too closely on curtains of falling water. Here I have tried to catch a waterfall in situ. The mist in the valley, the bark peeling off the trees, the waterfall highlighted in a frame of green— everything contributes to an air of freshness and mystery.

The Garden State

For its size, it is amazing what is packed into Victoria. It is like a treasure chest full of riches: the diamonds of Wilson's Promontory and the Great Ocean Road; the sapphires of the Otway Ranges and Croajingolong National Park; the emeralds of the Grampians and the Alpine National Park. There are even some unpolished opals: Mt Arapiles, a mecca for rock climbers from around the globe, and the sandy, scrubby Mallee, the closest Victoria gets to outback.

Victoria calls itself the Garden State, and there is definitely something compact and neat about it, like the formal gardens spread around the capital, Melbourne.

Personally I prefer the rambling feel of the country garden I found one day in the Mirranatwa valley, south of the Grampians, where the plants have evolved their own distinctive order rather than had one imposed on them.

Victoria is the most densely-populated state, with two-thirds of its people living in Melbourne. Like country dwellers everywhere, those in Victoria tend to look on the "Big Smoke" with distaste. But the city dwellers love the country and ensure that the state's 31 national parks and 46 state parks are among the nation's most visited.

Because it is so small, I believe Victoria needs to be even more protective of its wilderness areas. The rainforest of Tarra Bulga National Park is one of its most amazing jewels, but was nearly lost amid plans to harvest its timber. People need to draw strength from the bush. For the second most populous state to lose more wilderness would be as ridiculous as the state with the second most cars dismantling its petrol stations.

From the banks of the graceful Murray River where I was born, to the high country where you can gaze across hundreds of kilometres of thick forest and alpine terrain, we would be immeasurably poorer without Victoria's natural heritage.

These rainforest falls are among the loveliest I've ever seen: a blade of water slicing through a gully thick with ferns and trees weeping down over the banks. Anybody who has walked through a rainforest, absorbing its atmosphere and symmetry, knows how it recharges your spirit. It is like a great outdoor cathedral filled with beauty and awe.

Previous Page
The Twelve Apostles, Port Campbell

Burnished by the glow of the setting sun, half of the famous Twelve Apostles loom up out of an uncommonly placid sea. Although they have withstood centuries of pounding waves, these huge limestone pillars, like the towering cliffs behind them, are being slowly whittled away. In fact, only ten of the original twelve now remain standing, their two brothers having been martyred at the hands of water, wind and time.

With only rocks, grass tussocks and button wildflowers for company, Craig's Hut looks out in every direction across hundreds of kilometres of solitary wilderness. Built for the film The Man from Snowy River, this replica of an early settlers' slab hut stands today as a memorial to the high country men and women whose fierce love for the land taught them they could respect it and work it but never tame it. They have a lot to teach us today.

Every feature of these distinctive snow gums, from their contorted limbs to their brash streaks of colour, speaks of character. These trees have stood firm against everything that's been thrown at them—wind, rain and snow. Often the only way to acquire character is by weathering storms.

Waves churn past the sole surviving arch of London Bridge, a natural wonder that only a few years ago lost a second span connecting it to the mainland, toppled by the incessant onslaught of the ocean.
A tourist caught on the formation at the time had to be lifted off by helicopter. How easy it is for people to put their trust in things that seem permanent but aren't really permanent at all!

Above
"Gateway to Heaven", High Country

It's only an old lopsided gate—or is it? A sky of awesome power entices and the way is open, beckoning. Are you game to step into the unknown?

Right
Dogman's Hut, headwaters of the Murray River

A mixture of corrugated iron, rough-cut poles and river stones, this old cattlemen's hut still provides overnight refuge for people travelling in the high country. While the cattlemen who built it are no longer permitted to graze their stock in highland areas, other adventurers keep the hut's fires burning, including the owner of the saddles seen here—a rider who was chasing wild brumbies (bush horses).

Left
Tidal River Beach, Wilson's Promontory National Park

A tender sea caresses the beach of Norman Bay, coating its fine sand with a film of moisture and making it shine like polished marble. "The Prom", as it is known to countless thousands of holiday-makers, is the southernmost point of the Australian mainland and one of the country's most popular National Parks. Granite outcrops typical of the peninsula stand impressively in the vivid orange sunset.

Previous Page
"Rolling Hills", Johanna

These undulating green hills always remind me of Psalm 23: "The Lord is my shepherd, I shall not want. He makes me to lie down in green pastures, He leads me beside the still waters." Amazingly, this tranquil scene was photographed in the middle of a roaring gale, and that too is symbolic for me: sometimes in the roaring and buffeting of life we need to lay down and rest and allow Someone far bigger than us to take control.

Right
Sunrise and mist over Omeo Valley

A sylvan valley stretches and yawns as the sun rouses it from sleep. The night has been cold, but above the blanket of mist a golden hill stands as a promise of the warmth of day.

Overleaf
Pendergast Court, Benambra

The lengthening shadows of late afternoon stretch out to wrap around an old abandoned homestead in eastern Victoria. Once a prominent local property, Pendergast Court belongs to an era that is passing like the dying day, and what its place in the day to come will be is hard to say. A remnant of the past, it sits, quiet and dignified, awaiting an unknown future.

Previous Page
Big Tom's Beach, Murray River, Cobram

*A faint vibration ruffles the surface of the Murray River, blurring the
reflections of the tall gums that bask in the soft-hued aura of sunrise.
Here on this stretch of white river sand, half way between Albury
and Echuca, I relive childhood memories of growing up on Australia's
biggest waterway: Sunday afternoon picnics, awkward little
homemade canoes, and boyish dreams of swimming the mighty river
to prove myself a man.*

Above left and right
Hopetoun Falls, Otway State Forest

Water as smooth as velvet glides over moss-coated rocks in the Aire River. Seen here from the same vantage point facing left then right, this secluded gully typifies the profusion of life that fills the temperate rainforests and eucalyptus bushland along Victoria's south-west coast. It is a tragedy that so many of these sanctuaries have been lost—and a greater tragedy that we are continuing to let them slowly disappear under the chainsaw's blade.

Left
Wallace Hut, Falls Creek

In winter these gnarled snow gums stand in a field of white, but here the early morning spring sun has broken through after a brisk night to warm the sap of the trees and the blood of any hikers who happen to be sheltering in Wallace Hut. An old cattlemen's shelter, in winter it provides refuge for cross-country skiers from the perils of blizzard and black night.

Overleaf
Sunset over paddocks, Mansfield

After three tiring days shooting in the high country, I was on my way out for a nice, quiet dinner when the sky abruptly exploded overhead. Suddenly I was catapulted into action, frantically trying to keep up with the rocketing light. After ten minutes it was over, and I was left standing breathless in the middle of the field, overwhelmed by God's pyrotechnic extravaganza. You never know when glory may catch you unawares; you just have to be ready.

NORTHERN TERRITORY

The Outback

If the presence that dwells in the Australian landscape has a centre, it is Uluru. In the arid heart of Australia, at the junction of the continent's four greatest deserts, God has placed a monument to His creative genius that encapsulates all that is unique about this land.

In 1985, Uluru and the area around it were handed back to the Anangu people who inhabited the region before whites came. To stand beneath Uluru is to feel what they have always known: how small we human beings are, and how privileged we are to call this country home.

But Uluru is only the best-known of the Northern Territory's natural marvels. The Territory is an outlandish, wonderful, awe-inspiring place. You see it in the landscape: the riot of tropical vegetation in the Top End, the red dust and eerie rock formations of the Centre. You experience it in the climate: the 45°C (113°F) days and freezing nights of the south, the exhausting humidity and deluging rains of the north. You see it in the wildlife: termites that build hills the height of houses and five metre (16 foot) long man-eating crocodiles.

The isolation and heat has rubbed off on the inhabitants, too, making them hardy and proudly individualistic. A spirit of comradeship binds them together, born of facing similar hardships.

Scattered throughout the Territory are the people originally entrusted with this continent, many of them trying to keep alive their traditional way of life. I have learnt a great deal from Aboriginal people. They understand the spiritual nature of reality in a way we European Australians have long forgotten. It's not something you can easily explain, but something you have to feel and flow with.

I believe the future of this nation is like a jigsaw puzzle. Black and white Australians each have some of the pieces, but we're only going to see the picture when the pieces begin to come together.

Left
Kurumpa, Mutitjulu, Uluru

Fascinating patterns sweep down the grainy sandstone flanks of Kurumpa, one of the innumerable twists and folds in the sides of Uluru (Ayers Rock). Many people visit Uluru to climb it or see its legendary colour change at sunset, but to really enter into its majesty you need to walk around it. At the base of the Rock, dwarfed by its unimaginable bulk, you truly feel how profoundly it is rooted in the land which gave it birth.

Previous Page
Jim Jim Falls, Kakadu National Park

A gorgeous veil of water plummets from the Arnhem Land escarpment, a sheer 215 metre (705 feet) drop into a deep plunge pool. At the height of the wet season, from November to March, these Falls become a torrent, with uncountable millions of litres raging into the gorge and detonating at the bottom in mighty clouds of spray. The dry season reprieve gives the area a chance to display its more benign side.

Right
Kakadu sunrise

Like a conductor waving a baton, a silhouetted tree raises its hands to begin the early morning Kakadu symphony. Deluged annually by up to 1600 millimetres (62 inches) of rain, the wetlands of Kakadu teem with bird life, from the tall, black-necked jabiru (stork) to the finch-like yellow chat. Each day a chorus of screeches, screams and whistles greets the sunrise, music for a transcendent ballet of clouds and sky.

Overleaf
Sunset, Kata Tjuta

Shadows creep into the valleys and ravines of Kata Tjuta as night approaches and the land prepares for the hush of darkness. Like Uluru situated 30 km (18.5 miles) to the east, this extensive maze of domes is an ancient focus of Aboriginal life and beliefs. To stand within its towering amphitheatre is to feel close to the heart of creation. Here, the late afternoon sun shoots beneath the clouds and illuminates its rich red tones.

Left
Anbangbang Gallery, Nourlangie Rock, Kakadu

Above and overleaf
Yellow Waters, Kakadu

Anbangbang Gallery shelters at the foot of Nourlangie Rock, an enormous sandstone mass that rises out of the flat Kakadu landscape like a misplaced piece of the Arnhem Land escarpment. With evidence of Aboriginal occupation dating back thousands of years, it is one of some 5000 rock art sites in Kakadu. Painstakingly rendered with ochres taken from the land, this frieze depicts ancient figures and testifies to the Aboriginal people's age-long pursuit of the realm of the spirit.

The wetlands of Kakadu are a kaleidoscope of colour. A gliding river (above), whose boundaries blend indefinably with the flood plains, displays a luminous spectrum of blue, while the same area at dawn (overleaf) is swathed in purple, with pink-tinged tree trunks and opulent green grass glowing in the misty stillness. During the dry season, algae in the shrinking billabongs gives the water a distinctive yellow tinge.

Above

Maggie Springs, Mutitjulu, Uluru

An iridescent rain trail leads down Uluru's side into this permanent pool on the southern side of the Rock. Such waterholes have supported human life here for millennia. When the rains come and the waters tumble down from fold to fold, this thin quiet pool becomes a flood. Water and the life it nourishes are deeply entwined with the Rock: even the name Uluru comes from the name of a waterhole near the summit.

If you travel down the Stuart Highway from Tennant Creek to Alice Springs, you'll soon come upon a strange collection of hundreds of boulders, some as big as houses, strewn across a spinifex valley in imposing and even impossible positions. Made of granite and rounded by erosion and flaking, their official name, the "Devil's Marbles", implies a diabolical origin—as if the devil had thrown them down with mischievous carelessness. I prefer to think of them as the handiwork of a Creator who does nothing haphazardly.

Left
Maguk Falls, Kakadu National Park

Crystal fresh water slides down a steep incline into an emerald pool, creating one of Kakadu's loveliest swimming holes. Ringed by pandanus palms and other rainforest vegetation, the deep pool has a sandy bottom and is free from the menacing saltwater crocodiles that make swimming elsewhere in Kakadu impossible. The dark swirls of tiny fish are visible in the shallows.

Right

The sleepy serenity of Florence Falls, Litchfield National Park, is broken by the first mauve light of dawn.

Overleaf

"Tears for a Nation", Uluru

A rare fall of rain sends water rushing down the gullies of Uluru, fresh and pure and white as the tears of God. I believe this photograph is prophetic for our nation. God is grieved by the terrible division between black and white, and here, in the very heart of Australia, we see His pain. The Spirit only works in unity. Australia will only fulfil its rightful purpose if we move together, putting aside our past and looking forward to our future. Our destiny is controlled by something far greater than race. We have to learn from each other.

An ephemeral but brilliant pillar of light flares across a cloud-darkened sky, transforming the dull, overcast mood of Kata Tjuta into a celebration of sunrise. Rearing up from the flat, scrubby sand plains typical of central Australia, the Olgas (as they are also known) are made from conglomerate, a mixture of pebbles and boulders cemented together by sandstone. The Aboriginal name Kata Tjuta means "many heads".

Among the many amazing engineers of nature, the termites of Australia's Top End mix earth with saliva to construct mounds that dry rock-hard in the sun. Reaching as high as 6 metres (19.5 feet) and honeycombed with innumerable passages and chambers, these wondrous insect metropolises are always aligned north and south—hence their designation "magnetic".

TASMANIA

The Holiday Isle

Tasmania is the home of wild light. The weather there is so changeable that on a recent trip I consulted the weather bureau daily before planning my itinerary. But it didn't work; they kept sending me towards predictable, and boring, blue skies. Back under the severe shadow of Cradle Mountain, I discovered that to capture the true Tasmania you have to go into the teeth of the storms and wait until the light breaks through.

Tasmania is a spectacularly beautiful state, with natural treasures so astounding that nearly a quarter of its area is listed as of World Heritage importance. An exquisite mountain and rainforest wilderness stretches the length of the state's west, while the midlands and eastern coastal fringes are rich with undulating, fertile countryside.

Pressured by geography, the population is concentrated on the northern and south-eastern coasts. Tasmanians are a friendly, winsome bunch, but they are definitely Tasmanians, not "mainlanders". They have a commitment to family ties and so-called "traditional" values that I find appealing. In manners as well as climate, Tasmania is closer than other states to the England from which its original settlers came.

The successful preservation of Tasmania's western wilderness has set a precedent for the whole nation.

Rather than further shredding the fabric of our land, the time has come to care for it with a passion. Still today, in Tasmania and elsewhere, the draconian practice of clear-felling is decimating irreplaceable forest. But these forests are the nation's future. They are what people will come from around the world to see for generations to come—not scraggly regrowth forests that lack all majesty or magic.

When I camp under a 500-year-old King William Pine, drinking in the peace of untouched wilderness, hope is rekindled in my heart that we can yet break with the past and fulfil our destiny as "The Great South Land".

Left
A gossamer cataract adorns multi-tiered Liffey Falls in Liffey Valley State Reserve.

Previous Page
Lake Elysia, The Labyrinth, Cradle Mountain-Lake St Clair National Park

A shadowed foreshore of grey rock and bleached trees forms a borderline between the dramatic heights of the Labyrinth and their mirror image in the near-motionless waters of Lake Elysia. With Mt Geryon on the left and The Acropolis on the right, this glacier-hewn valley is one of many hidden delights that lie off the well-worn hiking tracks in Tasmania's central highlands. Many people first discovered its stunning beauty through the work of the late Peter Dombrovskis (1945-1996), one of Australia's great landscape photographers, and I dedicate this photograph to him.

The pure blue of the morning sky is magnified in the icy depths of the Pool of Siloam. A group of five mountains around a scenic valley, the Walls of Jerusalem National Park has an aura of grandeur that leaves visitors in awe. There is a holy feeling here, a sense of Presence. It's no wonder the people who first mapped it chose biblical names.

Above and right
Sleepy Bay, Freycinet National Park

Rocks by the thousand line the shore of Sleepy Bay on the east coast, a treasure-trove of beauty profligately strewn around. I love the endless combinations of shapes, sizes, textures and smooth curves, all splattered with the jaunty red and yellow of lichen. Many of these rocks are boulder-sized, rounded by the scouring of the ocean. It's amazing what beauty can emerge when the rough edges are knocked off!

Overleaf
Lake Dove, Cradle Mountain

While Lake Dove is blanketed in somnolent grey, a shaft of dawn sunlight kisses the jagged top of Cradle Mountain. Skirted by rock walls gouged out long ago by vast fields of ice, the Lake is the northern starting point for the 80 km (50 miles) Overland Track which traverses the full length of Cradle Mountain-Lake St Clair National Park. In an area that is overcast eight days out of ten, when you catch a shot like this you realise it's a gift from heaven.

Right
Sunrise, Eddystone Point, Mount William National Park

The unflinching bulk of Eddystone Point provides a solid platform for a pink granite lighthouse, itself a bulwark against potential destruction for ships approaching Tasmania from the north-east. Built in 1887, its yellow pinprick of light conjures up the universal human fascination with lighthouses as a symbol of guidance and warning.

Previous Page
Pine Valley, Cradle Mountain-Lake St Clair National Park

Like learned scholars with long, flowing beards, pandini trees stand beside petite Cephissus Falls, discussing the wisdom of the timeless forest. Pine Valley is a magical land where trees many hundreds of years old grow in gullies thick with moss, and the memory of Eden still seems fresh and alive. We desperately need to preserve many more special places like this.

On a day of comparative calm, small waves skip along the rocks of one of western Tasmania's more accessible harbours. Along this treacherous coastline, it is more common to find giant swells pounding the shores and cliffs. I am always amazed at the resilience of the land to withstand the ocean's siege. It is fascinating to watch these rocks move against one another as the waves push them back and forth, as if they had learnt to roll with the surges rather than resist them.

Above
River Tamar, near Deviot

The Tamar River is a silken thread connecting Launceston with Bass Strait, flowing past orchards, vineyards, forests and pasturelands on its 64 km (40 miles) journey to the sea. Here around Deviot is wine-making country, and as the night draws in a solitary boatman savours the intoxicating silence of the river at evening.

Above
Sunset, south of Trial Harbour

Wild light leaps up from the horizon and plays among the clouds as the setting sun prepares to pull down the curtain on another day. Far below, the waters of the Southern Ocean twist and turn like a dancer determined to whirl until the last note of music dies away.

Its timbers greyed by rain and snow and furious winds, Mt Kate hut stands as an enclave in a world that runs by laws often inhospitable to human beings. Built in the mid-1940s as part of a private logging operation harvesting King William Pine, it is now protected as a cultural heritage asset and is only used as occasional accommodation for Parks and Wildlife Service staff. Cradle Mountain looms in the distance.

Under a seething sky, the smooth, geometric curve of Wine Glass Bay provides a haven for a handful of grateful mariners. Viewed here from the top of nearby Mt Amos, the Bay and the bulbous Freycinet Peninsula are bathed in the silver glow of dusk. Each December, participants in the annual Sydney-to-Hobart yacht race end up here for post-race celebrations, but this photograph shows a unique wilderness enjoying the last memory of the day's light with a minimum of human intrusion.

Bound together by luminous pastel tones, the ocean, land and sky blend seamlessly in a picture of serene harmony. Sheltered from the stormy winds that make weather so unpredictable further west, the island's east coast is a slow seaside world and much sought-after holiday destination. But the chill of evening sends most visitors indoors, and the area returns to its blissful seclusion.

Photographer's Notes

People often contact me asking for photographic advice, so here I would like to share a few thoughts that may help you capture better images.

I do not presume to tell anyone how they must take photographs. I believe we all see differently, which is what gives each of us our unique style. When we follow our brain we are limited by our own understanding, but when we follow our heart we tap into a bigger picture.

Having said that, I think there are a few tips I can pass on. I think you'll love the first one.

BREAK THE RULES

The bottom line is: There are no rules. If an image works, it works; if it doesn't, it doesn't.

At one of my exhibitions, a person with a doctorate in photography was looking at one of my shots and I could see she was puzzled. I asked if I could help. "I can't believe this!" she replied. "This guy has the horizon in the middle. It should be one-third sky, two-thirds foreground. But this really works!" The person didn't know I was the photographer, so I simply replied, "Isn't it lucky he doesn't know the rules, or this shot may never have happened."

There's only one rule that is a must: Make sure you have film in your camera. Although I once met a photographer who sometimes left the film out because he wanted to enjoy the privileged position of being a photographer without being disappointed with the results!

STOP TALKING AND START TAKING

One of the hardest parts of photography is getting out of bed. Just stick a film in your camera and get on with it.

If you're going to eat an elephant, the way to do it is one bite at a time. If you sit back and look at how big the elephant is, you'll never finish the tusk at hand. If you had a dream to shoot a book on Australia, you could think "What a huge place!" and be so overwhelmed that you never begin. Or you could pick somewhere to start and attack it one bite at a time. If you persevere, you'll reach your goal through committed action.

LOOKING PAST THE I

The biggest thing blocking the light is often your own shadow. We often get so locked into what we want to achieve or why we have gone to a particular area that we miss the very thing we are there for.

I believe there is a force at work which is much bigger than you or I. The key is to tap into the Creator's power rather than your technical understanding, which by comparison is very limited. This is a hard pill for many to swallow (especially "techno heads") because people love to be in control. Personally, I would rather be out of control. I'm just an average photographer with a great God.

I have definitely not perfected this area of relinquishing control, but I'm working on it. Wow, it's exciting! How small we are and how big He is.

USING WHAT YOU HAVE

If you're not using what you already have, you won't use what you think you need. Many think they need a really good camera to take photos, and sure, it's nice to have a great camera. But the way to get it is by using the one you've got.

I started taking photos on my Dad's old Praktica, and my first book, *The Last Frontier*, was shot using only two second-hand Widelux cameras. Talk about equipment with limitations—only three shutter speeds and constant breakdowns! But they did the job. The best understanding of your equipment comes from using it.

The technical aspects of a shot are secondary to capturing the spirit of a moment. Some years back, at my sister's bidding, I judged a junior school photo competition. Some of the work was good; some was average. But there was one landscape shot which was just awesome. It had been taken at sunset by an eight-year-old boy using a disposable camera, through the window of a bus, travelling at 100 km (60 miles) per hour. Against all odds, this shot really worked. It sure humbled me.

WILD LIGHT

Light is absolutely one of the most important things to consider. No light, no photograph!

Different light conditions suit different subjects. For example, overcast light may not work for a summer beach shot, but it is great for rainforests, especially during or after light rain. Early morning and late afternoon is usually the best time to take photographs as the light has great warmth and softness. Uluru (Ayers Rock) doesn't actually change colour; it's the changing colour temperature of the light that makes it appear so radiantly red at sunset.

One thing to be careful of is a 'blue sky mentality'. In Australia we are blessed with lots of blue skies, and this can sometimes become boring in photographs as the sky often takes up a large part of an image. Cloudy light or wild, moody light can test your patience, but when the breaks happen you can get great emotion in a shot. Times of wild light are when I often speak to God, asking (respectfully!) such things as, "What are you up to?" or "Come on, give me a break—please!"

THE THIRD DIMENSION

Photography is a two-dimensional medium, so we sometimes need to try to create a third dimension in our photographs—especially in landscapes—to give depth to the images.

A simple way to do this is to use strong foreground interest. Another way is to use lines within the shot to draw the viewer in—a road, a fence, a curve of the beach. Sometimes a good way to get better depth in a shot is to shoot from a higher vantage point. I often take shots from the top of my car, or standing on my camera case.

PASSION

Passion is like an artesian well—when tapped, it brings life and energy to even the most barren desert. Passion, like attitude, is contagious and is essential for a project to succeed.

Life is an adventure, not a worry, and if you want to pursue a dream, stumbling blocks must become stepping stones. Passion is a powerful thing, and when directed properly it can help you bring visions to reality.

One question I often ask myself is "Why am I doing this particular project?" I believe the motive should have a greater purpose than mere selfish gain. When people say, "I want to be a photographer, like you", I say, "Why?" I think we should be constantly asking ourselves this question. My goal and passion as a photographer is to show the beauty of God's creation so that people may look beyond self.

PATIENCE

Photography is like fishing. The most beneficial part is learning to relax while you wait and get into the rhythm of what is happening around you. The fruit that keeps you going is that occasional big catch—a good photo.

Patience is a discipline (shocking word), and when we learn to be still, blessings come our way. Once I was shooting in America at Yosemite National Park, and I waited all day for the light to be what I considered 'just right'. Throughout the day, about five other professional-looking photographers came along. Each one pulled out his mega-expensive camera, tripod, the works, waited a couple of minutes, then went click, click and left. Meanwhile, I was still waiting, waiting, waiting and wondering if in fact I had missed something.

Finally, right at the end of the day, when all seemed beyond redemption, the light began to dance and the scene came alive. I was the only one still there, and I believe I caught the big fish. I hope they enjoyed their sardines!

TECHNICAL ASPECTS

Surround yourself with the best support

Having good suppliers is a key to great results. If they are the best in their fields, then you won't have to worry about that particular aspect of your photography. Here are contacts I highly recommend for various aspects.

FOR EQUIPMENT SUPPLY: L & P Photographics Ph:(02) 9906 2733
They are true professionals with a great understanding of the photographic industry.

FOR PRINTING: CFL Print Studio Ph:(02) 4365 1488
The best Ilfochrome (Cibachrome) printers in the world. They also process E6 film.

FOR FRAMING OR MOUNTING: CFL Framing Studio Ph:(02) 4367 8499
They know how to mount professional photographic prints properly.

The equipment I use

• I use a Nikon F90 for my light meter. Previously, I used a spot meter and the zone system, but I prefer to make it easy for myself as well as grab a few 35mm shots along the way.
• My main camera is a Linhof 617S which has a 90mm lens. It uses 120 roll film and it gives me four shots to a roll. The transparency size is 6cm x 17cm. There is no better fixed lens panorama camera than Linhof. Nearly all my images on this camera are shot from a tripod, except aerial work.
• I also use Noblex cameras, both PRO 6/150U (120mm roll film) and 135U (35mm roll film). They are the best of the rotating lens panorama cameras. They give great depth of field and are easily hand-held.

• I use a Linhof tripod with ball head and quick release mounts. It is quick to use which helps with urgent shots.

The film I use

I use Fuji film exclusively because for me it's the only film that captures the true colours of Australia. I try other films as they come on the market but nothing comes close to Fuji Velvia, my preferred film.

The vehicle I use

Toyota is the only vehicle I trust for serious four-wheel driving in this country. As a bonus, Toyota has the best service backup throughout Australia. My Toyota Landcruiser knows that if it ever does break down it will get a serious talking to, because I hate all that grease and mechanical stuff and do it only under duress. Driving sure beats walking, and breaking down in the outback can be dangerous.

The communication I use

Telstra is my choice of communication companies. Firstly, because no other company has the coverage or range of services Telstra provides. Secondly, as an Australian I want to support those who have helped make this great country what it is today. I constantly use Telstra Payphones, phone products and VHF radio services. Phonecards are ideal for those who move around a lot and when you don't have sufficient coins for payphones. PhoneAway is a must for the traveller either making contact with those overseas or when travelling overseas. Telstra's Payphones and card products can be used anywhere, anytime to keep in touch.

Financial Services

We all need a bank capable of thinking outside the square. I have been with *Colonial State* through various growth phases since 1970. Their faith in my vision over the years has enabled me to capture the beauty of this great nation.

Index